Spies, Lies
& Books

James Whinray

Bossiney Books

Author's neurosis

Do I known enough about espionage to write this book?

To the best of my knowledge I have only ever met two spies. The first was Anthony Blunt, during the time when his guilt was known to the authorities, but not to the public, myself included. The circumstances were a little odd, and I was surprised by how suspicious of me he seemed, but the meeting only lasted a couple of minutes and was inconsequential.

The second was at the Frankfurt Book Fair, where I was manning a stand. A Russian came and sat down, soon revealing that he knew nothing about the book trade and then that a year or two previously he had been turfed out of the Russian embassy in London in a tit-for-tat operation. We dutifully laughed together at how absurd it was to think that he was ever a spy.

The Fair, attended by thousands of book trade people from all over the world, must have been ideal cover for meeting contacts, but quite exhausting for an ageing spy walking round between assignations. Seventies tradecraft presumably suggested that you spot an empty chair, start chatting, and hope to be offered a beer.

Is that enough??

First published 2019 by
Bossiney Books Ltd, 67 West Busk Lane, Otley, LS21 3LY
www.bossineybooks.com
© 2019 James Whinray   All rights reserved
ISBN 978-1-906474-72-0

Acknowledgements

The cover photograph is by Robert Hesketh, www.roberthesketh.co.uk

Printed in Great Britain by R Booth Ltd, Penryn, Cornwall

Introduction

Spies can be of many kinds. Internationally there are spies 'on our side' and spies against us. Each side consists of undercover agents working in a foreign country and spies at home trying to identify and neutralise the other side's agents. And there may well also be spies at home, operating on behalf of the government against those of its own citizens who may disagree with the government's policy. In Britain this has happened intensively at certain nervous moments of our history, for example the Elizabethan period, the French Revolution (which it was feared would be imitated in Britain) and during the first world war. The government at each of these times appeared to be suffering from paranoia. Which is normal if you fear for your country.

Sometimes private organisations become involved in spying. Their motive may be political, in the belief that their government is not doing enough to protect the nation's interests, or their obsession. And of course it may be industrial espionage, which has not been covered in this book.

Max Schultz and his Doppelgänger

Even the cleverest spy is in danger of being caught, but we assume they will have at least some 'tradecraft' to minimise the risk. Early in the twentieth century, however, both in Britain and Germany, conspicuous heroics were the sign of an officer and a gentleman. One German spy seems either to have lacked any training, or perhaps to have decided that brazenness was the best policy: he pretended to be a journalist.

In 1911, Max Schultz moored a yacht called the *Egret* at the mouth of the the Yealm. He was a 31-year-old with a doctorate in philology, who had come to Britain ostensibly to teach languages in Plymouth – perhaps with a view to recruiting young naval officers as agents.

He was engaging in a little gun practice on his boat when he accidentally shot his housekeeper. She intended to sue him, so he approached a Plymouth solicitor, Samuel Hugh Duff, to act in his defence. (They had possibly already met in Dartmouth, where Duff happened to be the managing director of the Palladium cinema.)

Duff had connections with the dockyard in Plymouth as well as in Dartmouth, and according to a report of his trial Schultz began to ask a series of blatant questions 'regarding the preparedness of the British Fleet in case of any sudden developments of the Moroccan crisis'. In much the same way, he approached Duff's contact Edward Charles Tarren. (In the 1911 Census, Duff was a visitor staying with Tarren who was described a cash register salesman.) Schultz offered both of them contracts as correspondents for a German newspaper. Both pretended to accept, and then fed Schultz false information provided by the British security services.

A police investigation showed that Schultz had visited other important naval sites, at Woolwich, Chatham and Portsmouth, which he readily admitted. While in Portsmouth on his 'houseboat' (the *Egret*?) he had flown the German flag and thrown parties at which he tried to get the guests talking about naval matters.

He was tried in Exeter: Duff acted as prosecutor. The defence was that the information Schultz was seeking was not detrimental to national security, and that such information was already printed in British newspapers. To which the prosecution response was that he was seeking authentic information, whereas what was published in the papers was false. Schultz was sentenced to 21 months.

By a strange coincidence (assuming it was coincidence) a British spy also named Max Schultz was arrested in Germany in the same year. This Max Schultz was born in Hull, the son of immigrant parents, and had become a ship owner – 'oil contractor' in the Census, so perhaps importing petroleum from Europe. He had been running agents in Germany, including an engineer who supplied very useful battleship blueprints, and he was sentenced to hard labour.

In Hull Maritime Museum there is a model ship he made while in prison, in the funnel of which he hid a tiny scrap of paper explaining that he made the model to help pass the time, 'having been sentenced in Leipzig to seven years for espionage for the dear old English government'. Meanwhile Max Schultz's wife and five children were living in Hull: in 1915 and again in 1917 there were anti-German riots there in which anyone with a remotely German-sounding name was at risk, and the mob duly smashed the windows of our hero Schultz's house.

Max returned after the war, though not immediately: he had been given a new job, recruiting agents to stir up trouble within the German navy. That kind of life has its perils. He died of alcoholism in 1924 – having changed his name to Hilton, his wife's maiden name.

Guy Burgess

Now to a more famous spy. Guy Burgess was born in Devonport in 1911. His father, Malcolm Kingsford de Moncy Burgess, was a rather unsuccessful naval officer, his mother the daughter of a wealthy Portsmouth banker. He was destined for Dartmouth Naval College. Aged 9, he was sent away as a boarder to the most expensive preparatory school in England, after which he spent a gap year at Eton. In September 1924 his father died of a heart attack while making love. According to Guy, he had to pull his father's body off his mother. (Burgess always liked a good story, and if the Oedipus complex exists, then he certainly had it, so this may not actually be true.)

Aged 13 1/2, he entered Dartmouth Naval College. Life at the prep school had been pretty tough, with one master described as a sadist who liked hitting boys on the head; but it was nothing to Dartmouth, which was run like a Victorian naval vessel. There was severe discipline, total uniformity, and everything had to be done 'at the double' to the accompaniment of shouts and threats. Beatings could include the cat o' nine tails.

Guy Burgess was very bright, excelled academically and was more than adequate on the sports field, but he hated the place and rebelled internally. He was found to have poor eyesight, so there was no chance of an active naval career: life in a naval administrative job was no attraction, so he returned to Eton. (Andrew Lownie in his excellent book *Stalin's Englishman* says that 'poor eyesight' at the Naval College was 'often a euphemism for dishonesty or homosexuality' and used as an excuse to be rid of unsuitable boys.)

At Eton he was something of a loner, not particularly popular, bumptious and increasingly left-wing; he was again academically successful and won a scholarship to Trinity College, Cambridge. His Eton history teacher, the eminent historian Steven Runciman, described him as 'An interesting mind but rather undisciplined. He was a type that Eton sometimes produces – the Young Revolutionary.'

Left-wing he might have been, but Burgess was incredibly vain and remained proud of having been at Britain's top school. An Eton and Cambridge contemporary (and there were an awful lot of old Etonians at Cambridge in those days) said 'My lot generally regarded him as a conceited unreliable shit.' At Trinity he met both Kim Philby and Anthony Blunt, with whom he shared artistic as well as other interests.

Many young people at the universities were radicalised by the economic events of 1929-32 when unemployment in Britain reached 3.5 million, with many more forced to work part-time, and also by the Nazi violence which was already well under way in Germany – not to mention its would-be imitators in Britain.

Quite a few students concluded that capitalism had failed, as Marx had predicted, and communism seemed the only antidote. In such times of crisis it is unsurprising if some young people – especially those brought up to see themselves as natural leaders – find wringing of hands insufficient and leap at active alternatives, some to the right and others to the left. In the 1930s many students became idealistic socialists, and some joined Communist Party cells. The Cambridge University Socialist Society had 200 members, of whom a quarter were also members of the Communist Party of Great Britain.

Blunt introduced first Burgess then other communist sympathisers to the Apostles, an elitist and highly secretive philosophical club founded in 1820, whose members included John Maynard Keynes, E M Forster and Bertrand Russell. Burgess and Blunt seem to have used their membership of the group for recruitment, certainly of Michael Straight (see page 9) but other names have also come under suspicion.

Burgess got a first in Part One, but collapsed while taking his Part Two exams, despite, or perhaps because of, taking drugs to keep himself going. He was given an *aegrotat* – an unclassified degree awarded to a student who would have passed the exams if fit enough to take them. Burgess visited Russia in 1934, and on his return warned that conditions there were far from the perfection which propaganda suggested – but the fact that foreigners couldn't get things right was surely no reason to abandon an idealised principle for his own country.

By this time Kim Philby had been recruited to the Soviet spy network, and produced a list of seven potential agents, of whom Maclean was top of the list, and Burgess last because 'his character is that of an *enfant terrible*'. However, the Soviet intelligence service thought the fact that Burgess was a flamboyantly promiscuous homosexual could be of great advantage to them.

Homosexuality was illegal in Britain at the time – indeed until 1967 and even after that except in private. Active homosexuals were always in danger, and consequently had their own tightly knit networks. They were liable to blackmail, so a spy within such networks could potentially be very effective – as Burgess proved to be. Guy Burgess's activities were so very blatant, as were those of many other Etonians, and yet they did so little damage to his career in the BBC, the civil service or the intelligence services, that one wonders whether there was an unwritten law that Etonians were not subject to prosecution: he invariably wore an old Etonian tie, even when otherwise dressed like a tramp, both for snobbery and perhaps to warn off officious cops. On one occasion when he was caught soliciting, he somehow escaped prosecution.

So Burgess was recruited by Russia; he promptly resigned from the Party and pretended to have done a political U-turn, now infiltrating right-wing Conservatives who were Nazi sympathisers.

Burgess had hoped for an academic career, but was unable to complete his PhD. Instead he began working for the BBC in the Talks Department, subsequently producing 'The Week in Westminster', which of course made him sought after by MPs. Before long he was also recruited by MI6, so his career as a double agent had begun – though in his mind there was never any doubt that loyalty to communism came first.

Over the next decade Burgess was employed in various sensitive posts in the Foreign Office. Both as private secretary to Hector McNeil, a member of the Cabinet and Ernest Bevin's deputy as Foreign Secretary, and in the 'Information Research Department', he was able to take top secret documents home and photocopy them.

He produced so much information for the Soviets that his expenses claims to them include purchase of a suitcase in which to deliver the material. In the first six months of 1945 alone he supplied them with

389 documents classified as top secret. The Russians could not keep up with translating it all.

But it was not only the documents which were useful to the Russians. Burgess seems to have known everybody, whether in politics or the arts, and gossip provided him with much useful material. He was notoriously entertaining, often scandalous, and good company – though many people commented that he was incredibly slovenly, with filthy clothes and dirty fingernails, that he chain-smoked and drank heavily all the time. He also abused prescription drugs, sometimes obtained from a friendly vet. He was a notorious liar, so perhaps most people did not believe him when he said loudly in public that he was working for the Russians, as he quite often did when drunk. His fellow pro-Russian spies complained about his indiscretions.

The Foreign Office and Hector McNeil were less amused by his antics than were his nightclub friends. In May 1950 Burgess was posted to Washington, which he accepted only reluctantly. His new colleagues decided he was a useless drunkard and the ambassador steadily demoted him. Both his health and his morale were rapidly deteriorating and he was in self-destruction mode. On one day he was caught speeding three times, but claimed diplomatic immunity. It was decided to send him home in disgrace.

Kim Philby by this time was the head of MI6 in Washington, and had a tip-off that Maclean was likely to be uncovered any moment. Burgess was instructed on his return to Britain to warn Maclean, and arrangements were made for Maclean's 'exfiltration'. In the event, and without Philby's knowledge, Burgess decided to accompany Maclean, and the two of them left England on 25 May 1951. This brought Philby under suspicion, and before long he was forced to resign with a golden handshake; there was only circumstantial evidence against him so he was not prosecuted.

Massive damage was caused to British-American relations by this affair. The American secret services could no longer trust their British counterparts, and it would be many years before even the British were (fairly) sure they no longer had moles in their own midst.

Burgess and Maclean disappeared for five years, before reappearing in Moscow. Burgess seems to have lived a lonely life in exile until he died aged 51 in 1962, the immediate cause of death being liver failure – hardly surprising given his lifestyle. He was known to say while living there that he didn't like Russian communists: British communists were much nicer. He remained convinced that a communist Britain would have been nothing like the Soviet state.

An article in 1955 discussing the Burgess/Maclean case in *The Spectator* was apparently the first to use the phrase 'The Establishment' to mean 'the whole matrix of official and social relations within which power is exercised' – and exercised socially as much if not more than administratively. The Establishment had an instinctive feeling for 'the right people', it recruited them, made allowances for peccadilloes, and hastened to cover up impeccably if things went wrong.

Burgess, Maclean and Philby were undoubtedly 'the right kind of people' – Eton and Cambridge, Gresham's and Cambridge, Westminster and Cambridge respectively – but on this occasion at least the Establishment, by ignoring every indication of problems, had got things hopelessly wrong.

Michael Straight

Guy Burgess was not the only member of the Cambridge spy ring with a Devon connection. Michael Whitney Straight (1916-2004) was the son of an American banker and his wife Dorothy Payne Whitney. They were among America's wealthiest couples.

His father died in 1918; his mother then married Leonard Elmhirst in 1925 and they purchased Dartington Hall, where Straight spent part of his childhood. He went to the London School of Economics before going to Cambridge, where he was recruited as a Russian spy by his lover Anthony Blunt.

On returning to the USA, Straight worked as a speechwriter for Roosevelt, then flew as a bomber pilot before taking over a family-owned magazine, and subsequently writing novels. When offered a government job in 1963, he voluntarily disclosed his spying activities, and it was this which led to the incrimination of Blunt (who had been long suspected) – but the Establishment decided the information was too embarassing, and it was not publicly acknowledged until revealed by Margaret Thatcher in 1979.

'M'

One does not expect to find 'MI5's greatest spymaster' as landlord of an Exmoor pub, but truth can be stranger than fiction. Charles Henry Maxwell Knight (1900-1968) was born in South London, the son of a solicitor. His father was a spendthrift, often hard up, and died in 1914, leaving the family dependent on a rich Welsh uncle.

Maxwell Knight was sent to a very tough school for merchant navy cadets, then took a job as a clerk. He had two obsessions, playing jazz and exotic pets. At one time he had a baboon, a bulldog and a bear. Work was perhaps less stimulating: he was fired by the Ministry of Shipping after just a year, causing his uncle to disown him. The next move was teaching games at a prep school. Then at the age of 23 he was recruited to an unpaid role by the Makgill Organisation, a private intelligence agency working mainly for industry, and aimed at subduing the Red Peril.

But Maxwell Knight was asked to infiltrate a quite different organisation, the British Fascisti, with a view to finding fellow spies to fight communism. He found 30, many of whom remained his friends for decades. The Fascisti were an extremist organisation, though rather less extreme than Oswald Mosley's later rival outfit, the British Union of Fascists, and they had a thug department enthusiatically run by Knight and his friend William Joyce (later to be famous as Lord Haw-Haw) which delighted in violent street battles with communists, as well as breaking and entering and 'trashing' left-wing offices. Knight was rather good at that.

He was also extremely good at recruiting and then handling agents and before long he was working for MI5, MI6 and Special Branch as well as for Sir George Makgill. Some discretion and juggling of information must have been required, but all the security services were in the 1920s concentrated on the communist threat, and saw the fascists as a necessary defence.

In 1925 Knight married Gwladys Poole, daughter of a wealthy retired army officer. She was an enthusiastic hunter, cricketer, and a leader of the British Fascisti, whose General Council had initially included more women than men. Knight did not let on that he'd joined as a spy, but by that stage he was enthusiastically behind the movement in his own right. However, when the General Strike was called off after a fortnight, it became obvious that there was not about to be a British Marxist revolution, and ordinary membership of the movement declined, leaving it open to its extremist fringe.

In 1927 Gwladys bought the Royal Oak pub at Withypool, as well as a long stretch of the River Barle, and she and Maxwell moved to Exmoor. She went off hunting, he went off fishing. Presumably they had staff to run the pub. The marriage was not working and it remained unconsummated. After two years Maxwell Knight returned to London except for weekends, while Gwladys stayed at Withypool.

Special Branch had been discovered to be full of moles, and both MI5 and MI6 were damaged too. MI6 took on Knight to run a fresh organisation, then there was a massive bust-up between the various agencies, which the Labour government resolved by banning MI6 from domestic work and giving that power to MI5 under Sir Vernon Kell – who made Maxwell Knight head of a special section with its own staff and offices. He decided to call himself 'M' and the section 'M Section'. In practice its HQ was M's flat, pets and all, and he maintained a distance from the rest of the organisation.

When Oswald Mosley started the BUF in 1932, M joined. When the government decided that fascism was as much a danger as communism, M was very slow to react. He didn't really believe it.

In 1936 Gwladys went from Withypool to London to do her Christmas shopping. She stayed not with M but at a club of which he was a member, and somehow she took an overdose of drugs from which she died two days later. Was it suicide? Was it an accident? Was it even, as some of her family suspected, murder? Or had M at the very least driven her to it? The inquest returned an open verdict.

M would later marry twice more, and in both cases the marriage remained unconsummated. A secretary/agent in a memoir after his death described him as both gay and homophobic, though he liked the company of women. In those days, it was quite common for homosexual men to marry in order to prove to society, and sometimes to themselves, that they were 'normal', and the result was not infrequently distressing.

There was much publicity following Gwladys's death, and it could have damaged M's career: instead of a loveable jazz-playing, pet-keeping eccentric, journalists could just as easily have portrayed him as a rather weird fascist sympathiser with an interest in the occult, a friend of Aleister Crowley.

But soon after this M had his first great success, breaking a Russian spy ring that was stealing plans from the Woolwich Arsenal. Then, after war had broken out, he uncovered another spy ring with a mole in the US Embassy, who was passing transcripts of Churchill and Roosevelt's conversations to Mussolini. The agent who penetrated that plot was Hélène de Munck, a Dutch national for whom M secured British citizenship, and who after the war ran a Devon guesthouse. She died at Barnstaple on 1 April 1964, when her address was given as Old Court, Berrynarbor.

So M became something of a (secret) hero. Let's forget that in 1939 he tipped off William Joyce that he was about to be arrested, and instead celebrate the arrest of Mosley and other fascists who were preparing to collaborate with a German invasion.

Among the agents M recruited were Eric Roberts (see below) and David Cornwell (see page 28). There is no space here to give his exploits (or even his eccentricities) in full. Apparently he features as Jack Brotherhood in John Le Carré's *A Perfect Spy*, and of course he features at least in name as James Bond's 'M'.

He retired from the secret services in 1961, but already before that he had begun a new career – writing numerous nature books and pet-keeping guides, such as *How to keep a Gorilla* and *Be a Nature Detective*. He seems to have found running agents rather similar to keeping pets. As 'Uncle Max' he endeared himself to children with his broadcasts for BBC radio. What a strange man he was!

Eric Roberts

Eric Roberts (1907-1972), one of Maxwell Knight's most successful agents, was from a Cornish family with its roots in St Keverne. In 1911 the family lived in Penzance, where Eric's father worked for the Western Union Cable Company as a 'cable operator and telegraphist'. (Western Union had a cable station in Trewithen Road, with an underground link to Sennen Cove where the transatlantic cable came ashore.)

Roberts was recruited by M in 1925, aged 17, when he was a member of the British Fascisti. He was persuaded to resign from the Fascisti and infiltrate their opponents the Communist Party, which he did very successfully.

On the outbreak of war he acquired a new role. By that time he had married, was working as a clerk for the Westminster Bank in Euston Road and was commuting from his family home at Tattenham Corner near Epsom racecourse. He seemed a totally innocent suburban nonentity, and his managers at the bank were perplexed. 'What we would like to know here is what are the particular and especial qualifications of Mr Roberts – which we have not been able to perceive – for some particular work of national military importance which would take him away from his normal military call-up in October?'

They were not given an honest answer. Eric's new role was to pretend to be a Gestapo agent, to identify Nazi sympathisers in the UK, and extract from them information which they would be convinced was going to Germany. The information which he was able to intercept would, among other things, have given Hitler construction plans of British jet engines and knowledge which would have 'rendered our radio location system completely useless'.

The extent of the treachery he exposed shocked the secret services: Roberts came up with nearly 500 names, and found that successful German bombing raids were actually applauded by these Nazi sympathisers.

In doing this undercover work, Roberts seems to have been emotionally reliant on Maxwell Knight. He used the alias 'Jack King', whilst M used the alias 'Captain King'. And Eric named his first son Maxwell.

After the war Eric Roberts was moved away from M and assigned to MI6, first to deskwork, then a year in Vienna, where his job was to pass accurate but low-value information to a Russian agent – 'chicken feed'. He felt this work was undemanding (though extremely dangerous) and grew depressed. He tried to warn his colleagues about Soviet moles in the service, one of whom he knew was called 'Tony' (actually Anthony Blunt) but the response was hostile. Roberts felt that as a grammar school boy he'd never been accepted by the toffs who ran the service. During an interview, 'I made the biggest blunder of my career. I said that if the Soviet agent became a member of one or two of the most exclusive clubs, I doubted if anybody would be willing to entertain doubts of his loyalty.' This was shortly before the exposure of Burgess and Maclean, later Philby and finally Blunt.

It is hard to believe, but in 1956 Eric Roberts was found 'unsuitable for intelligence work' and left the service. He was convinced that he was himself under surveillance, which caused him great stress and depression, and he emigrated to Canada. At no point before his death was his enormous contribution before or during the war ever acknowledged, even by a quiet word from 'the Office'.

Frank Foley

If the Cambridge spy ring depressed you, perhaps this next item will cheer you up. Frank Foley (1884-1958) was born in Highbridge on the Somerset coast, the son of a railway locomotive fitter from Tiverton. He was educated at Stonyhurst College, then went to a Catholic seminary in France, but decided against becoming a priest. He became fluent in both French and German. During the war he was commissioned in January 1917 and commanded an infantry company.

Because of his language skills, he joined the Intelligence Corps in 1918 with the task of recruiting agents in the Netherlands, Belgium and France. Subsequently he became a passport control officer in Berlin, but his real job during the 1920s and 1930s was to recruit and run agents who could report on German military research and re-armament. As passport control officer, he was able to disobey the rules and enable thousands of Jews to escape from Germany, obtaining visas for them from both the UK and other countries, in the process visiting internment camps and even sheltering Jews in his own house – a highly dangerous activity considering that he had no diplomatic immunity.

During WW2 he helped run the network of agents in the Double Cross System, and after the war he was responsible for hunting former SS war criminals.

Counter-espionage in Somerset

There is a curious association between spies and writers and it goes back a long way – though alas, Christopher Marlowe had no West Country connections! In 1797 the Government was alerted to suspicious activity in Somerset. We are fortunate to have an exact record. A Dr Lysons in Bath wrote to the Home Secretary, the Duke of Portland on 11 August 1797:

> My Lord Duke – On the 8th instant I took the liberty to
> acquaint your Grace with a very suspicious business
> concerning an emigrant [immigrant] family, who have
> contrived to get possession of a Mansion House at Alfoxton,
> late belonging to the Revd Mr St Albyn, under Quantock
> Hills. I am since informed, that the Master of the house has
> no wife with him, but only a woman who passes for his sister.
> The man has camp stools, which he and his visitors take with
> them when they go about the country upon their nocturnal
> or diurnal excursions, and have also a portfolio in which they
> enter their observations, which they have been heard to say
> were almost finished. They have been heard to say they
> should be rewarded for them, and were very attentive to the
> river near them – probably the river coming within a mile or
> two of Alfoxton from Bridgwater. These people may possibly
> be under agents to some principal at Bristol.
>
> D Lysons

On the same day a detective, who had already been despatched towards Bath to investigate, reported from Hungerford to the Home Office:

> Sir — Charles Mogg says that he was at Alfoxton last Saturday
> was a week, that he there saw Thomas Jones who lives in
> the farm house at Alfoxton, who informed Mogg that some
> French people had got possession of the Mansion House and
> that they were washing and mending their cloaths all Sunday,
> that he Jones would not continue there as he did not like it.
> That Christopher Trickie and his wife who live at the dog-
> pound at Alfoxton, told Mogg that the French people had

taken the plan of their house, and that they had also taken the plan of all the places round that part of the country, that a brook runs in front of Trickie's house and the French people inquired of Trickie whether the brook was navigable to the sea, and upon being informed by Trickie that it was not, they were afterwards seen examining the brook quite down to the sea. That Mrs. Trickie confirmed everything her husband had said. Mogg spoke to some other persons, inhabitants of that neighbourhood, who all told him they thought these French people very suspicious persons and that they were doing no good there…

As Mr. Mogg is by no means the most intelligent man in the world, I thought it my duty to send you the whole of his story as he related it.

I shall wait here your further orders and am Sir, your most obedient humble servt.

G Walsh

To which his boss replied the very next day:

Sir – I have considered the contents of your letter to me from the Bear Inn, Hungerford, of yesterday's date. You will immediately proceed to Alfoxton or its neighbourhood yourself, taking care on your arrival so to conduct yourself as to give no cause of suspicion to the inhabitants of the Mansion House there. You will narrowly watch their proceedings, and observe how they coincide with Mogg's account and that contained in the letter from Mr Lysons to the Duke of Portland.

Should they however move, you must follow their track and give me notice thereof, and of the place to which they have betaken themselves. I herewith transmit you a bank note of £20.

J King

On 15 August Walsh reported from the Globe Inn at Stowey:

Sir — In consequence of your orders which I rec'd yesterday, I immediately set out for this place, which altho' it is five miles from Alfoxton, is the nearest house I can get any accommodation at. I had not been many minutes in this house before I had an opportunity of entering upon my business, by a Mr Woodhouse asking the landlord, if he had seen any of those rascals from Alfoxton. To which the landlord reply'd, he had seen two of them yesterday.

Upon which Woodhouse asked the landlord, if Thelwall was gone. I then asked if they meant the famous Thelwall. They said yes. That he had been down some time, and that there were a nest of them at Alfoxton House who were protected by a Mr Poole a Tanner of this town, and that he supposed Thelwall was there (Alfoxton House) at this time. I told Woodhouse that I had heard somebody say at Bridgwater that they were French people at the Manor House. The landlord and Mr Woodhouse answered, 'No, no. They are not French, But they are people that will do as much harm as all the French can do.'

I hope tomorrow to be able to give you some information, in the mean time I shall be very attentive to your instructions. I think this will turn out no French affair, but a mischiefuous gang of disaffected Englishmen. I have just procured the name of the person who took the house. His name is Wordsworth, a name I think known to Mr Ford.

I have the honor to be Sir, your most obedient humble servt

G Walsh

and on the following day, 16 August:

Sir —The inhabitants of Alfoxton House are a sett of violent Democrats. The house was taken for a person of the name of Wordsworth, who came to it from a village near Honiton in Devonshire, about five weeks since. The rent of the house is secured to the landlord by a Mr Thomas Poole of this town. Mr Poole is a tanner and a man of some property. He is a most violent member of the Corresponding Society and a strenuous supporter of its friends. He has with him at this time a Mr Coldridge and his wife, both of whom he has supported since Christmas last. This Coldridge came last from Bristol and is reckoned a man of superior ability. He is frequently publishing, and I am told is soon to produce a new work. He has a press in the house and I am informed he prints as well as publishes his own productions…

By the direction on a letter that was going to the Post yesterday, It appears that Thelwall is now at Bristol.

I last night saw Thomas Jones who lives at Alfoxton House. He exactly confirms Mogg of Hungerford, with this addition, that the Sunday after Wordsworth came, he Jones was desired to wait at table, that there were 14 persons at dinner, Poole and Coldridge were there, and there was a little stout man with dark cropt hair and wore a white hat and glasses (Thelwall) who after dinner got up and talked so loud and was in such a passion that Jones was frightened and did not like to go near them since. That Wordsworth has lately been to his former house and brought back with him a woman servant, that Jones has seen this woman who is very chatty, and that she told him that her master was a phylosopher…

Your most obedient humble servt

G Walsh

We also have the poet Samuel Taylor Coleridge's own account of the affair, written twenty years later:

The dark guesses of some zealous Quidnunc met with so congenial a soil in the grave alarm of a titled Dogberry of our neighbourhood, that a spy was actually sent down from the government *pour surveillance* of myself and friend. There must have been not only abundance, but variety of these 'honourable men' at the disposal of Ministers for this proved a very honest fellow. After three weeks' truly Indian persever-ance in tracking us (for we were commonly together), during all which time seldom were we out of doors but he contrived to be within hearing (and all the while utterly unsuspected: how indeed could such a suspicion enter our fancies?) he not only rejected Sir Dogberry's request that he would try yet a little longer, but declared to him his belief that both my friend and myself were as good subjects, for aught he could discover to the contrary, as any in His Majesty's dominions.

He had repeatedly hid himself, he said, for hours together behind a bank at the sea-side (our favourite seat) and over-heard our conversation. At first he fancied that we were aware of our danger, for he often heard me talk of one Spy Nozy [Spinoza], which he was inclined to interpret of himself, and of a remarkable feature belonging to him, but he was speedily convinced that it was the name of a man who had made a book and lived long ago. Our talk ran most upon books, and we were perpetually desiring each other to look at this, and to listen to that, but he could not catch a word about politics. Once he had joined me on the road (this occurred as I was returning home alone from my friend's house, which was about three miles from my own cottage) and, passing himself off as a traveller, he had entered into conversation with me, and talked of purpose in a democrat way in order to draw me out.

The result, it appears, not only convinced him that I was no friend of Jacobinism, but (he added) I had 'plainly made it out to be such a silly as well as wicked thing, that he felt ashamed though he had only put it on.'

I distinctly remembered the occurrence, and had mentioned it immediately on my return, repeating what the traveller with his Bardolph nose had said, with my own answer; and so little did I suspect the true object of my 'tempter ere accuser', that I expressed with no small pleasure my hope and belief that the conversation had been of some service to the poor misled malcontent.

This incident therefore prevented all doubt as to the truth of the report, which through a friendly medium came to me from the master of the village inn, who had been ordered to entertain the Government Gentleman in his best manner, but above all to be silent concerning such a person being in his house. At length he received Sir Dogberry's commands to accompany his guest at the final interview; and, after the absolving suffrage of the gentleman honoured with the confidence of Ministers, answered, as follows, to the following queries.

D: Well, landlord! and what do you know of the person in question? Has he not been seen wandering on the hills towards the Channel, and along the shore, with books and papers in his hand, taking charts and maps of the country?

L: Why, as to that, your honour, I own I have heard – I am sure I would not wish to speak ill of anybody, but it is certain that I have heard —

D: Speak out, man! don't be afraid, you are doing your duty to your King and Government.

L: Why, folks do say, your honour, as how he is a Poet, and that he is going to put Quantock and all about here in print; and as they be so much together, I suppose that the strange gentleman has some consarn in the business.

So ended this formidable inquisition.

Coleridge, who wished to downplay his own radical youth, is putting a spin on the event, making it a case of rustic idiocy appropriate for the comedy scenes in a Shakespeare play, but there is more to it than that.

In 1797 Britain was at war with France. The French were intending to invade Ireland, and simultaneous diversionary attacks were planned on English or Welsh targets. The French had attempted to land at Bantry Bay in December 1796, just nine months before the Alfoxton events, but were forced back by bad weather. Then in February 1797 four French naval ships carrying 1200 soldiers, dressed in British uniforms and with Irish officers, had sailed up the Bristol Channel and been observed passing Ilfracombe, but had again been foiled by the wind, and diverted to a beach in Pembrokeshire, where the invaders landed, but were soon out-numbered. The French vessels had rapidly departed in search of prizes, and the 1200 invaders surrendered without a fight.

So the Government had good reason to be suspicious when there was a report of strangers (initially thought to be foreigners because the locals couldn't understand the Wordsworths' northern accents) making 'plans' (presumably landscape sketches) of an area known to be targeted by the French. And even when the supposed foreigners had been identified, they could not be ignored.

When the French Revolution began in 1789, it was seen with delight by many British people, who felt nearly as oppressed by the power of their aristocracy as did the French. Britain was in no way a democracy. Only a small proportion of men, and no women, had the vote, but even those who had votes were mostly unable to make a free choice. Both the American and the French examples gave them hope of change at home. As Wordsworth himself would write, looking back on his youthful self,

> Oh! pleasant exercise of hope and joy! …
> Bliss was it in that dawn to be alive,
> But to be young was very heaven!

The Government reacted to the French Revolution, and to the hopes of the British people that change was possible, by cracking down on freedoms of all kinds.

In 1797 Wordsworth and Coleridge were both still radicals and it is interesting that Wordsworth's name was 'known to Mr Ford'. Coleridge, who at one time aspired to be a Unitarian minister, had recently given a sermon in Bristol on the text 'When they shall be hungry they shall fret themselves, and curse their king and their God,' at which most of the congregation left in disquiet. If there had been a French invasion which appeared to be promoting British democratic reform, both men might well have supported it. After all, the Dutch invasion of 1688 which created the 'Glorious Revolution' was an excellent precedent – though by 1797 both men had become aware that the French Revolution had not led to the utopia they had anticipated.

As for John Thelwall, who was a guest at William and Dorothy Wordsworth's dinner party, he was a leading member of the London Corresponding Society, which argued in a very responsible manner for democratic reform of the electoral system and was therefore thought highly dangerous by the Government. At this time of Government paranoia, Thelwall (who had a reputation for 'volcanic' oratory) and two other leading members had been tried for treason, but acquitted; he was still regarded as the most dangerous man in Britain and was hounded wherever he went. As a result of the Seditious Meetings Act (1795) he had ceased to lecture on modern politics, and instead lectured on ancient Rome, quietly drawing obvious comparisons.

Contemplating this curious episode, I am impressed by the calm and reasonable approach of the detective, G Walsh, who sensibly decided that the poets were not a serious threat, and persuaded his superiors that this was the case.

D H Lawrence

Wordsworth and Coleridge were by no means the last authors to be suspected of espionage, but D H Lawrence is perhaps unique, having been accused of spying by both German and English police.

In 1912 he was holidaying in Germany with his future wife, born Frieda von Richthofen (a very distant cousin of the flying ace the Red Baron) who was still married to the academic Ernest Weekley. He wrote to a friend:

> I had to quit Metz because the damn fools wanted to arrest me as a spy. Mrs [Frieda Weekley] and I were lying on the grass near some water – talking – and I was moving round an old emerald ring on her finger, when we heard a faint murmur in the rear – a German policeman. There was such a to-do. It needed all the fiery little Baron von Richthofen's influence – and he is rather influential in Metz – to rescue me. They vow I am an English officer – I – *I!* The damn fools.

They married in 1914, and when war broke out they were not permitted to leave England but Lawrence had TB so was not subject to conscription. He was intensely and vocally opposed to the war, and with a German wife inevitably came under suspicion. Rather like Coleridge, Lawrence had a dream of founding a utopia, perhaps in Florida, or some other foreign land. He wrote in 1915 to Lady Cynthia Asquith (daughter-in-law of the prime minister: he may have been the son of a coal miner but he did not lack contacts) shortly after her brother had been killed:

> In this war, in the whole spirit which we now maintain, I
> do not believe. I believe it is wrong, so awfully wrong, that
> it is like a great consuming fire that draws all our souls up
> in its draught. So if they will let me I shall go away soon, to
> America. Perhaps you will say it is cowardice: but how shall
> one submit to such ultimate wrong as this which we commit
> now, England – and the other nations? … I feel like a blind
> man who would put his eyes out rather than stand witness to
> a colossal and deliberate horror.

Very understandable to us, with hindsight, but not a popular view
at the time. He was not permitted to leave Britain. The nearest he
and Frieda could get to Florida was to move to Cornwall, firstly to
Porthcothan near Padstow, then to Higher Tregerthen, an isolated
cottage near Zennor. Various of his artistic friends visited them there,
including John Middleton Murry and Katherine Mansfield, and the
composer Philip Heseltine (a.k.a. Peter Warlock).

The Scottish composer Cecil Gray took a cottage three miles away at
Bosigran. While Frieda apparently had a fling with Gray, Lawrence had
a 'friendship' with a local farmer, William Henry Hockins. The novel
Women in Love was largely written during their time at Tregerthen.

Many of the locals found this Bohemian set rather hard to take. It
was not only that Lawrence sounded off about the horror of the war,
while their sons were sent away to do the fighting, and that Frieda was
a German, and moreover a haughty aristocrat, but that they received
German newspapers and sang 'German' songs. These may well have
been German *lieder*, but it is known that when with Gray the couple
sometimes sang Hebridean folk-songs – and the Gaelic was mistaken
for German.

Then Gray was fined £20 – a large sum in those days – for showing
a light at night. Atlantic convoys passed along the Cornish coast, and
the authorities feared possible signalling to enemy submarines. Very
soon after that, Lawrence wrote again to Lady Cynthia Asquith:

> Now comes another blow. The police have suddenly
> descended on the house, searched it, and delivered us a

notice to leave the area of Cornwall, by Monday next… This bolt from the blue has fallen this morning: why, I know not, any more than you do. I cannot even conceive how I have incurred suspicion – have not the faintest notion. We are as innocent even of pacifist activities, let alone spying of any sort as the rabbits in the field outside. And we must leave Cornwall, and live in an unprohibited area, and report to the police. It is very vile. We have practically no money at all – I don't know what we shall do…

They have taken away some of my papers, – I don't know what. It is all very sickening, and makes me very weary.

The papers included the words of the Hebridean 'Seal Woman's Song', which were suspected to be an encryption.

Lawrence later wrote a novel, *Kangaroo* – not his best work, but it does contain a fascinating highly autobiographical chapter describing this event.

Away in the West Richard and Harriet lived alone in their cottage by the savage Atlantic. He hardly wrote at all, and never any propaganda. But he hated the war, and said so to the few Cornish people around. He laughed at the palpable lies of the press, bitterly. And because of his isolation and his absolute separateness, he was marked out as a spy… He still believed in the constitutional liberty of an Englishman.

'You know,' said Harriet, 'you do say things to these Cornish people.'

'I only say, when they tell me newspaper lies, that they are lies.'

But now the two began to be hated, hated far more than they knew.

Hatred? Or just an understandable fear of 'strange' people? The Lawrences were not alone: in 1915 the great Scottish architect and designer Charles Rennie Mackintosh and his artist wife were ejected from their holiday cottage at Walberswick in Suffolk. His Glasgow accent was mistaken for German, and his wonderful pencil sketches of flowers were mistaken for plans of the local rivers – the full irony of which will be fully understood only by cryptic crossword addicts.

(But to be fair to the suspicious, Baden Powell had just published *My Adventures as a Spy*, revealing that he actually did disguise plans of fortifications as drawings of butterfly wings.)

Henry Williamson (1895-1977)

The author of *Tarka the Otter* experienced the hell of World War I before moving to Georgeham in North Devon and becoming a full-time writer. He was desperate to ensure that there should be no more wars, and believed that 'Hitler was essentially a good man who wanted only to build a new and better Germany'. He believed that wars began because of financial interests, which, for him, meant 'the Jews'. So he joined the British Union of Fascists in 1937. He was one of those who (see page 13 for Eric Roberts's comments) applauded the bombing of the banking areas of the City of London – they were 'purified by fire'.

In 1936 he had left Devon and bought a run-down farm at Stiffkey in Norfolk with a view to following the BUF's agricultural policy. The locals mistrusted him – he had not been popular in Devon either – and in June 1940 he was arrested and spent a weekend in a police cell at Wells-next-the-Sea on suspicion of spying, and inevitably of signalling to the enemy, but was soon released.

After the war he left the farm and returned to Georgeham, writing numerous books and remaining an unrepentant fascist – but in all probability not a spy.

Agatha Christie

Is no West Country author to be free from suspicion?

Actually Agatha Christie's time spent in the Middle East with her archaeologist husband Max Mallowan would have been excellent cover for espionage, and she did produce a spy adventure novel based on her experience, *They Came to Baghdad*, as well as several crime novels set in Syria, Iraq and Egypt. But if she did patriotic work for Britain in her spare time there, this has never been revealed. However, her next spy novel caused a commotion in MI5.

N or M? was published in 1941, featuring her pair of detectives

Tommy and Tuppence – who have never caught the popular imagination like Hercule Poirot and Miss Marple. The book apparently showed a considerable knowledge both of tradecraft and of the suspected 'Fifth Column' of traitors within Britain, and featured a character called Major Bletchley. At that time Bletchley Park was top secret, and it so happened that one of Agatha Christie's friends, Alfred 'Dilly' Knox, was a leading cryptographer there – fitted for the role by his academic life decoding papyruses.

Could it be that the choice of name was a playful joke by the author? MI5 approached Knox, who agreed to ask his friend casually how she'd chosen the name Bletchley. She told him that she'd got stuck at Bletchley Junction on her way by train from Oxford to London and took revenge by giving the name to one of her least lovable characters. Which apparently satisfied MI5.

But how did Agatha Christie come by her background knowledge for this book? The answer may lie in Lawn Road, Hampstead, where Agatha and her husband moved in 1941 into a modernist block of flats called the Isokon building, which is still there. It was an extraordinary block in many ways, home at various times to Walter Gropius, founder of the Bauhaus, Henry Moore, Nicholas Monsarrat, author of *The Cruel Sea*, Raymond Postgate, originator of *The Good Food Guide*, Philip Harben, the TV chef, and many other luminaries.

This was a time when Greenway House had been requisitioned, and Max and Agatha's other houses were at risk of bombing. They were introduced to the building by an old friend, Egyptologist Stephen Glanville, who was working for RAF Intelligence. Hampstead was not immune to bombing, but Glanville would have known that steel-framed concrete structures, of which there were very few at that time, were much safer than other buildings. The Isokon was one of the safest houses in London.

And Glanville was not the only resident to be aware of this. There were large numbers of European political refugees, many of them communist sympathisers and quite a few of them Soviet agents. At their centre was the disarmingly named Edith Tudor-Hart, who recruited Kim Philby in 1934. The agents might well have been tipped off that the Isokon building was, in more ways than one, a safe house.

According to David Burke, a spy historian who has devoted an entire book to *The Lawn Road Flats*, 32 suspected Soviet agents lived there or were regular visitors to Lawn Road in the 1930s and 1940s, which was surely not a coincidence.

While Agatha was there, those agents included Arnold Deutsch, who recruited and controlled the Cambridge Five, and Jurgen Kuczynski and his wife. He was a major in Soviet Intelligence. Kuczynski's sister also lived there: as 'Ruth Buerton' it was she who passed nuclear secrets from Klaus Fuchs to the Russians.

The Isokon building had been designed to be a social space – there was a popular bar with music and dancing and also a restaurant. It is quite probable that Agatha Christie knew the Kuczynskis and others. Her regular bridge partner was her next-door neighbour, Vere Gordon Childe, an Australian Marxist archaeologist. Whilst it seems unlikely that the conversation in the bar often turned to tradecraft, perhaps Agatha Christie picked up some interesting information from her socialising.

Unless, of course, she really was an old hand from the Middle East…

'Rebecca'

At least Daphne du Maurier was never suspected of spying – though her famous novel *Rebecca* was used by the Kondor Mission, an attempt to help Rommel invade Egypt. (Books can be used as the basis of codes, provided both sender and recipient have the same edition.)

In 1942 a spy named Eppler, whose father was Egyptian and mother German and who operated under the name Hussein Gaffar, was living on a houseboat in Cairo. He was aided by a belly-dancer who enticed British officers to the houseboat, where she entertained them while Eppler surreptitiously went through their papers. Within the houseboat was a cleverly designed radio unit disguised as a gramophone. The operator was totally concealed and could send messages in morse code to Rommel's army, while music was playing in the boat.

But the belly dancer was not the only woman regularly visiting the houseboat. A Jewish woman known as 'Yvette' spotted a copy of *Rebecca* together with a sheet of notepaper covered with grid squares

Bletchley Park

Alan Turing was educated at Sherborne School, but otherwise had no West Country connections. Less famous though probably equally important is Gordon Welchman (1906-1985), born in Bristol, the son of a missionary who had returned to become an Anglican vicar, and later archdeacon of Bristol. Welchman was a mathematician and a fellow of Sidney Sussex College, Cambridge. He and Turing were among the early recruits at Bletchley Park, and they worked together on the 'bombe' code-breaking machine. Welchman was head of Hut 6, whose task was to break German army and air force Enigma codes.

In 1948 he moved to the USA to initiate America's first computer course at MIT, and became a US citizen in 1962. He later wrote *The Hut Six Story* which was published in 1982, much to the annoyance of the security services, who removed his security clearance, which caused him great distress.

and letter groups, which she realised was a cipher. She immediately informed MI6, and the spies were quickly arrested.

The codebreakers at Bletchley Park had before long broken the code, and Field Marshal Montgomery was in a position to impersonate Eppler, deceiving Rommel about his army's movements, which resulted in the first military victory of the war at El Alamein.

'John le Carré'

It is extraordinary how many twentieth century spies also wrote novels. Apart from 'John le Carré' (real name David Cornwell), Ian Fleming, Graham Greene, and Maxwell Knight who wrote a couple, they include Somerset Maugham, John Bingham (the original for le Carré's George Smiley), Dashiell Hammett, and more recently Stella Rimington.

As Muriel Spark (who worked for British Intelligence but not as an agent) put it, 'The art of fiction is very like the practice of deception.'

The travel writer Patrick Leigh Fermor wrote some of his first published works at Easton Court Hotel, Chagford. During the war he had been for two years an agent in German-occupied Crete, disguised as a shepherd. He and a team of resistance fighters dramatically abducted the German military governor! Leigh Fermor wrote only one novel, but his travel writing, especially the books devoted to his 1934 walk as a maverick teenager from Holland to Istanbul, written decades after the event, is often more concerned with subjective intensity than with verifiable facts. He reimagined experiences, much like a novelist.

John le Carré's novel *A Perfect Spy*, which has a number of autobiographical elements, subtly touches on the similarities between creating a convincing espionage identity and writing fiction.

David Cornwell was born in Poole, Dorset, in 1931 and has had a cottage on the cliffs west of Lamorna in Cornwall since 1969. His grandfather had been a highly respectable alderman and mayor of Poole with a business specialising in the repair and painting of motor coaches, but David's father had rebelled against respectability and was a life-time criminal, a domestic abuser as well as a con-man, who knew everybody from Sir Donald Bradman to the Kray twins, lived an extraordinarily extravagant life without paying for it, and was imprisoned a number of times, in Zurich, Vienna, Jakarta and Singapore as well as in Britain.

David Cornwell seems to have been recruited by the intelligence services as a teenager, and later worked both for MI5 and MI6, running agents. The huge success of his third novel, *The Spy who Came in from the Cold*, enabled him to concentrate on his writing, frequently touching on the moral dilemmas involved in spying, but also addressing the tensions within the ruling classes of British society while it was adjusting to a post-war, post-imperial, world. *The Night Manager*, partly set in west Cornwall (though the filming location was near Hartland Quay), perhaps expresses a hope that the intelligence services are attempting to counter arms dealers who are at least as dangerous as foreign states.

My own favourite le Carré novel is *A Perfect Spy* which is about Magnus Pym, a double agent who at the end of his career is devoting himself to writing a confessional about his own duplicity and treacheries, which are the indirect consequence of his appalling father Rick.

Many of Rick's activities in the book mirror those of David

Cornwell's father Ronnie in real life. But in 'autobiographical' fiction, let alone that written by a former professional machiavel, it is a mistake to assume that everything is autobiographical simply because some of the obvious details are.

The book is also of interest for apparently containing a portrait of Maxwell Knight – Jack Brotherton in the novel – and for being partly set in south Devon.

Derek Tangye

By a strange coincidence, another author/spy lived just a mile from David Cornwell in Cornwall. In 1950 Derek Tangye (of a Cornish family) and his wife Jeannie shocked their friends by suddenly retiring from a social whirl in London, where he was a newspaper columnist and she the Press Officer of the Savoy Hotel, to run a smallholding on the cliffs above Lamorna growing early daffodils and potatoes. Derek then wrote a series of best-sellers about their life there called 'The Minack Chronicles'. During the war he had worked for MI5, his job being to gather potentially useful gossip from visitors.

In 2000 the *Mail on Sunday* claimed that secret documents in Moscow showed that Derek and Jeannie were double agents, collecting material on the private lives of the royal family and others which had potential for blackmail. The *Mail's* report was rubbished by most of the people who knew them in Cornwall. Nobody thought Derek had Communist sympathies – but then the motives of people who 'betray their country' can be very varied and often strange. Perhaps it was MI5 who told them to leave London. We'll probably never know.

Bampfylde Moore Carew

A notorious lover of disguise, and if he is to be believed a con-man even more prolific than Rick in *A Perfect Spy*, was Bampfylde Moore Carew (1690-1758). He was the son of Theodore Carew, Rector of Bickleigh, between Exeter and Tiverton, a member of a famous Devon family. He was the subject of *An Apology for the Life of Mr Bampfylde-Moore Carew*, and almost certainly supplied the facts for it, possibly even dictating it himself to the Sherborne publisher's wife – the facts and/or the fiction, because the book makes much play of comparing its protagonist to Fielding's Tom Jones, hero of the novel which had just been published in 1749.

The tone is often ironic, and there are frequent indirect comments on British politics, some anti-monarchical.

Carew went to Blundells School in Tiverton, but ran away to avoid punishment when he was 15, apparently joining a group of 'gypsies', though they were not Romany but a gang of vagrant beggars. Much of the book is repetitive, with endless accounts of Carew persuading people that he was a wounded war hero (giving recipes for faking wounds) or a shipwrecked mariner, or the victim of a fire.

Carew claims an almost miraculous ability to deceive anyone by disguising his clothing, accent or manner, and drops the names of just about every gentleman in the West of England, claiming to have deceived each of them in turn and been given a 'contribution', about which they can all have a good laugh when he reveals himself later. But he doesn't return the contributions.

His fellow beggars apparently think him a genius for his clever tricks. One hates to think what genuinely disabled people and wounded soldiers thought of a man who suggested they were all frauds, totally dependent as they were on charity in those days long before the welfare state.

Another feature of the book is an account of his travels to North America (as a convict), to Ireland, the Baltic, etc. Sometimes here the tone is almost that of a guide book, but often with ironic moralising, for example about the Native Americans:

> Here, Reader, it will be necessary to remark, that as our hero is no longer among the simple and honest Indians, who are not enough polished to forget the dictates of Nature, but follow her in all their ways; who have not art enough to deceive, but speak what they think and act what they say: as he is no longer amongst such, but amongst a polished people, whose knowledge has taught them to forget the ways of Nature, and to act every thing in disguise… we hope it will be no disgrace to the hero if among such he appears as polished as the best, and puts on a fresh disguise as often as it suits his conveniency.

So fraud is OK because all modern society is a con? It is tempting to think the whole book is a fiction, but there is evidence that Carew *was* sentenced to be transported to Maryland, where he would have been a slave for seven years, though it is not certain that he was ever shipped.

Checking the odd name or fact also makes one doubt. Certainly some are unlikely, for example the claim that he went to Edinburgh and then Carlisle to cheer on Bonnie Prince Charlie; Charles only took Carlisle on 15 November 1745 and Carew and his family were arrested as vagrants in Sherborne, Dorset, on 21 November.

But he claims to have been illegally dragged aboard a convict ship at Topsham, the ship being the *Philleroy*, Captain Simmons; and on at least one occasion the *Philleroy*, under Captain Peter Symons of Exeter, did indeed take convicts to Maryland, arriving in April 1742. Of course, that doesn't necessarily mean that Carew was on board.

Similarly, he claims to have sought out in Philadelphia a George Boone from Bradninch, and there really was a school teacher of that name and origin in Philadelphia, born in the same year as Carew, so perhaps they had been school-fellows in Tiverton.

The book is probably a racy mixture of fantasy and fiction, but there's little doubt that Carew was himself a dangerously amoral egoist and self-aggrandiser. No twitter account though.

Princess Caraboo

Most spies are 'watchers', perhaps pretending to political opinions the opposite of those they really hold (which must be hard enough) but otherwise being themselves. A very small number adopt an entirely false identity and background, not for an hour or two at a time like Bampfylde Moore Carew, but for months or years on end. They have no script to fall back on, but are dependent on their wits to cope with the unexpected. Perhaps there are some personalities to whom this is almost a necessity – and if they don't get the opportunity to play a false role in real life, they write fiction.

But what if they are poor and uneducated – can they still deceive the world? The following narrative appeared in a book published in 1817, *Caraboo: a Narrative of a Singular Imposition... by a young woman of the name of Mary Wilcocks alias Baker alias Bakerstendht alias Caraboo, Princess of Javasu.*

On Thursday evening the 3rd of April 1817, the Overseer of the Poor of the parish of Almondsbury in the county of Gloucester called at Knole Park, the residence of Samuel Worrall, Esq. to inform that gentleman and his lady, that a young female had entered a cottage in the village, and had made signs that it was her wish to sleep under its roof; but not speaking a language which its inhabitants or the Overseer understood, the officer thought it right to refer to Mr Worrall, a Magistrate for the county, for his advice; knowing also, that there was a man servant residing in Mr Worrall's family who was conversant with several foreign languages, and who could probably comprehend that in which the stranger spoke.

The female was in consequence ordered to be brought up to Knole Mansion, but to which removal she showed signs of strong reluctance; and when there, refused for some time to enter its doors. After some entreaty, she was prevailed upon to go in, and was presented to Mr and Mrs Worrall; who, with their servant, were unable to understand the language in which she addressed them; but intimated to her by signs, that they wished to ascertain, whether or not she had any papers in her possession; upon which she took from her pocket a few halfpence, with a bad sixpence, and implied, that she had nothing else. She had a small bundle on her arm containing a very few necessaries, and a piece of soap pinned up in a bit of linen. Her dress consisted of a black stuff gown, with a muslin frill round the neck, a black cotton shawl on her head, and a red and black shawl round her shoulders; both loosely and tastefully put on, in imitation of the Asiatic costume; leather shoes and black worsted stockings.

The general impression from her person and manners was attractive and prepossessing. Her head small; her eyes and hair black; forehead low; nose short; complexion a brunette; her cheeks faintly tinged with red; mouth rather wide; white teeth; lips large and full, under lip a little projecting; and her chin small and round. Her height about five feet two inches. Her hands were clean, and apparently unaccustomed to labour. No ear-rings, but the marks of having worn them. Her age appeared about twenty-five.

After a short consultation, Mr and Mrs W. deemed it most advisable to send her for the night to a public house in the village; and as Mrs W. felt much interested by her apparent distress, she ordered her own maid and footman to accompany her, it being late in the evening, and to request that the landlady would let her sleep in a private room, and provide her with a good supper and a comfortable bed; and that Mrs W. would call upon her early the following morning.

The young woman seemed much fatigued, and walked with difficulty. Upon being shown into the parlour of the public house, she was particularly struck with a print on the wall, representing the Annana [pineapple] and made those present understand it was a fruit of her own country, the representation of which afforded her much pleasure. Upon some preparation being made for her supper, she expressed a wish that she preferred tea; and before she partook of it, she covered her eyes with her hand, and appeared to repeat a prayer, bowing her head at the conclusion. Upon a second cup of tea being poured out, she refused taking it, until the cup was thoroughly washed; and when she had drunk it, she repeated the same form of prayer with much seeming devotion. When shown to the room in which she was to sleep, she appeared reluctant to go to bed, and pointed to the floor; but upon the landlady's little girl getting into the bed, and making her understand the comfort of it, she undressed, and after kneeling, and appearing to say her prayers, she consented to lie on the bed.

At seven the next morning Mrs W. walked down to the public house, and found the stranger sitting by the fire, apparently very disconsolate, and as she thought with strong traces of sorrow and distress on her countenance, though she expressed much joy at the sight of Mrs W. and accepted with visible marks of gratitude a change of linen, which Mrs W. had brought for her. While her breakfast was preparing, the clergyman of the parish, who had heard of her arrival, came in, bringing with him several books, thinking it probable she might recognize some one of the countries described in the plates they contained; and upon looking them over, she gave the spectators to understand that she had some knowledge of the prints which were descriptive of China; but made signs that it was not a boat, but a ship which had brought her to this country.

Gaining very little information from this enquiry, Mrs W. determined to take her back with her to Knole, and keep her under her roof, till something satisfactory transpired concerning her; and upon being invited, she followed Mrs W., again exhibiting symptoms of reluctance and apprehension. Upon passing through the church-yard in her way to Knole, she tried if the church door was open, and seemed much disappointed to find it fastened. Upon her arrival at Knole, she was led to the housekeeper's room, where the servants were at breakfast; and observing some cross-buns on the table (it being Good Friday) she took one, and after looking earnestly at it she cut off the cross, and placed it in her bosom.

Upon Mrs W.'s return from church, she summoned the young woman before her; and fearful of imposition, she attempted to interest the stranger by addressing her in the following soothing and compassionate language: 'My good young woman, I very much fear that you are imposing upon me, and that you understand and can answer me in my own language; if so, and distress has driven you to this expedient, make a friend of me; I am a female as yourself, and can feel for you, and will give you money and clothes, and will put you on your journey, without disclosing your conduct to any one; but it must be on condition that you speak the truth. If you deceive me, I think it right to inform you that Mr W. is a magistrate and has the power of sending you to a prison, committing you to hard labour, and passing you as a vagrant to your own parish.'

During this address, the countenance of the stranger evinced an ignorance of Mrs W.'s intentions, at the same time, making it apparent that she did not comprehend what Mrs W. had said to her; and she immediately addressed Mrs W. in her unknown tongue. Mrs W. then attempted to ascertain her name, by writing her own upon paper, and placing it before her, and pronouncing it several times, and putting a pen in her hand, intimated her wish, that she would write her name; but this she declined, shaking her head, and crying Caraboo, Caraboo, pointing to herself. Upon showing her some of the rooms at Knole, she appeared delighted at seeing some pieces of furniture with Chinese figures, etc. upon them, making signs that they belonged to her country, or that she had been in the country from whence they came. At dinner she declined all animal food, and took nothing to drink but water, showing much disgust at meat, beer, cider, etc.

On the following day (Saturday) it was thought advisable to take her into Bristol to examine her before the Mayor at the Council House; where no discovery could be made of her country or language, or whence she came, or whither she was going. She was therefore in the regular mode of commitment of persons in such situations, taken to Saint Peter's Hospital, the receptacle for vagrants and the poor of the city of Bristol. Here she remained till the following Monday, and it is well authenticated, that during her continuance in this house she refused food of every description. On the Monday Mrs W. whose solicitude for the welfare of her strange and singular guest had rather increased than diminished, went to Bristol and visited her at the Hospital. Her friendless situation had in the interim become public, and several gentlemen had called upon her, bringing with them for-eigners of their acquaintance in the hope of discovering who she was.

At the Hospital, it is but justice to remark that the most humane attentions, which are allowed of by the house, were shown to the stranger. Finding she rejected the usual food, eggs and other delicacies were provided for her. But she was firm in her refusal of all kinds of nourishment; and she neither eat or drank, or slept on the beds of the Hospital, while she remained there.

Mrs W. still feeling a lively interest in her fate, determined upon again removing her, and had her taken to the office of Mr W. in Bristol, where she remained during ten days, under the care of Mrs W.'s housekeeper. Daily efforts were made to discover her language and country, but without effect. At last a foreigner of the name of Manuel Eynesso, a Portuguese from the Malay country, who hap-pened to be in Bristol, was introduced to her, and he declared that he could undertake to interpret her language. The tale this impostor pretended to extract from her was, briefly, that she was a person of consequence in her own country, had been decoyed from an island in the East Indies, and brought to England against her consent, and deserted. That the language she spoke was not a pure dialect, but a mixture of languages used on the coast of Sumatra, and other islands in the East. This Manuel Eynesso in short invented a story so plausible, and one so well suited to the imposition the girl had determined to practice, that Mrs W. was induced a second time to take her to Knole, intending to communicate the particulars of her history, as far as she could collect them, to some respectable individual at the East India House, and extend her protection to her till the truth of her story could be developed [unravelled].

She accordingly resumed her old apartment at Knole. And from the 3rd of April till the 6th of June, she not only ingeniously and most effectually contrived to deceive her benevolent hostess, her family, and their domestics; but she had the address to delude and highly interest numbers of visitants at Knole, who were eager and solicitous to examine and listen to the unknown foreigner. There was no one who took a greater interest in her fate and adventures, than one gentleman who had made several voyages to the East Indies, who was conversant with every creek and harbour in those seas, and well acquainted with the customs of China. This gentleman committed to writing the following particulars, either extracted from the girl at various times by signs and gestures; or as it now appears, in the warmth of his anxiety to discover her history, he most probably assisted her in the creation and composition of them.

That her name was Caraboo; that she was the daughter of a person of rank, of Chinese origin, by a Maudin, alias a Malay woman, who was killed in a war between the Boogoos (Cannibals) and the Maudins (Malays). That whilst walking in her garden at Javasu, attended by three sammens (women) she was seized by the people of a pirate prow, commanded by a man of the name of Cheemin, and bound hand and foot, her mouth also covered, and that thus she was carried off. That her father swam after her; and in pursuit shot an arrow, which killed one of her women who were taken on board with her. That she herself wounded two of Cheemin's men with her crease [kris] when she was seized; one of whom died, but the other was recovered by the justee (a surgeon). After eleven days she was sold to the captain of a brig called Tappa Boo; the brig sailing during the transaction; she being conveyed from one ship to the other in a boat. That after four weeks the brig anchored at a port, remained there two days, and having taken on board four female passengers sailed again, and in five weeks more anchored at another port, where the four females were landed; that they stayed three days, and then sailed for Europe, which she reached in eleven weeks.

Being near some part of the coast of England, in consequence of the ill usage she experienced she formed and carried into execution the resolution to jump overboard, and she swam to shore. That the dress she had on consisted of a gown worked with gold; a shawl on her head of the same description, which was exchanged by an English woman, the door of whose house was green; for which she gave her a black stuff gown, a cotton shawl, and several other articles; in which dress, after wandering about for six weeks, during which period she was frequently admitted into various houses, she found her way to Almondsbury.

Her father's country she called Congee (China) — her own island, from whence she was taken, she called Javasu, and that of her mother the Maudins (Malaya). She described her mother's teeth as being blackened, her face and arms painted, and that she wore a jewel at her nose, with a gold chain from it to the left temple; which decorations her mother wished to have adopted for her, but her father would not consent. That he had three more wives, and that he was carried on the shoulders of macratoos (common men) in a kind of sedan or palanquin, and wore a gold button in his cap, with three peacock's feathers on the right side of his head, a gold twisted chain round his neck, to which was suspended a large square locket of amber-coloured stone, set in gold. That she herself wore seven peacock's feathers on the right side of her head.

Upon giving her some calico, she made herself a dress in the style she had been accustomed to wear. It was very short in the petticoat, the sleeves uncommonly wide and long enough to reach the ground, but only half-scored up, and confined at the wrists. A very broad band round the waist, which she described as embroidered, as was the bottom of the petticoat; embroidery also was round the bosom, and round the open part of the sleeves. She wore no stockings, but open sandals on the feet with wooden soles.

She pronounced her father's name Jessu Mandu and her own Sissu Mandu which was afterwards changed to Caraboo in consequence of her father having conquered his enemies. That he had the command of soldiers, and that when any people approached him, they made their salam or obeisance on both knees, lifting the right hand to the right temple, and that they presented fruit in a dish balanced upon the points of their fingers, kneeling upon both knees to her father, and upon one to herself. That servants salam to a gentleman with the right hand to the head, to ladies with the left...

When shown the drawing of an idol, the object of worship at Prince's Island [Panaitan] she expressed the greatest abhorrence, and implied that she did not do so; but that she worshipped Allah Tallah; and that her mother told her, if she did as her father did, who prayed to an image, that she would be burnt in the fire...

That Tappa Boo's was a dark complexion; he had long black whiskers, and long black hair plaited down the back, and knotted at the end in a bow; that he wore a kind of sealskin cap, and an ear-ring in his right ear. That his brig had guns, but did not know how many; there were about 40 men, among whom was a justee (a surgeon); the vessel carried Spanish colours. The ladies who were passengers used to talk and write, but she could not understand them, neither did they understand her. That she was very ill after Tappa Boo bought her, for which she was cupped in the back of her neck, and bled in the arm and wrist; her hair also, which was extremely long, was cut off, and she was confined to her bed a considerable time. That her illness was occasioned by her crying and great unhappiness in consequence of her miserable and forlorn situation. She explained, that at the same time when Tappa Boo bought her of Cheemin, that he bought a bag of gold dust; and that the water was so shoal or shallow at Javasu, that a large vessel could not come near. She described the sails of Cheemin's boat as seamed up and down, and of a different shape from those of Javasu, which were of matting or rush; that the Chinese were made across with split bamboo sticks. Upon having a plate of the flags of all nations shown to her, she fixed upon the Venetian war as Cheemin's; the Spanish as Tappo Boo's, and the Chinese as her father's...

The gibberish language, in which she made herself understood, was aided in a very striking manner by gestures and animation of countenance, which it is impossible to describe; and singular to relate, that during the ten weeks which she resided at Knole and in Bristol, she was never heard to pronounce a word or syllable which resembled her native tongue.

Mrs W.'s housekeeper, who slept with her, never heard at any interval any other language or tone of voice than that which she first assumed. The servants once said in her hearing, that they would lie awake, to listen if she talked in her sleep; and on that night, and afterwards, she feigned to be asleep, and began talking her gibberish.

In returning from Bristol sometimes in Mrs W.'s carriage, she was so fatigued that she fell asleep; but Mrs W., though she awoke her suddenly, never found a word or a sound escape her, which could lead to detection. In the choice of her food she was also equally consistent and uniform, and affected much peculiarity and nicety.

She dressed every thing herself; preferred rice to bread; eat no meat, drank only water and tea. She was very fond of Indian curry, which she frequently dressed herself, and made very savoury. She refused a pidgeon (a 'rampue') that was dressed, but having a live one put into her hands, she cut off its head, which she buried together with its blood under the earth, and then dressed and eat the other part. Fish she served in the same way. She always said her prayers night and morning, and rigidly fasted every Tuesday; on which day she contrived to ascend to the roof of the mansion at Knole, frequently at the imminent peril of her life. Ablutions she was particularly fond of: she was once seen to plunge into a pond in Knole Park, and she regularly knelt down and washed her hands and face by the side of it. She was equally correct and clean in washing the utensils in which she eat and drank.

The tenants, and farmers, and their daughters about Knole and at Almondsbury grew very fond of her, and she often visited them with Mrs W.'s leave, but they never found her tripping or off her guard, either in her conversation or general manners, always observing the custom of washing her tea cup, etc.

One day she appeared to be highly exhilarated, and gave the servants to understand, that it was her father's birthday, and that he was forty-seven years old. During her stay she used to exercise herself with a bow and arrows, and made a stick answer to a sword on her right side, the bow and arrows slung on her left shoulder. She oftentimes carried a gong on her back, which she sounded in a very singular manner, and a tambourine in her hand, the sword by her side and a bow and arrow slung as usual, her head dressed with flowers and feathers, and thus she made it appear she was prepared for war. During her residence at Knole, she had heard people say that this was the custom abroad, and so she imitated it. Sometimes she would row in the boat in the pond at Knole, using the oars very dexterously.

She learnt her salams, or mode of greeting, from what she overheard; and from the observations of people who had been in the East, and who conversed with her, she appears to have modified her system of deception. One gentleman happening to observe, that if she was an Hindoo, she would make the salam with an inclination of the head and both hands gradually brought down from the forehead; and if a Malay, she would put her hands on the side of her head, she immediately put her hand on the right side to a gentleman; and on the left to a lady.

Mrs W. was one evening absent from Knole on the day of a wake in the parish, and on her return found her missing. The gardens were searched, and she was discovered sitting in a high tree, in which she explained herself to have climbed because all the females in the house had gone into the village and she feared contamination from the men. In the garden also she one day constructed an arbour as a temporary place of worship, which she sprinkled with water and threw her shawl over her head when she knelt to prayers. She never omitted a grace at any of her meals.

Mr P. of Cathay, in the city of Bristol, a gentleman who had visited Malay several years since, was supposed to be able to throw some light on the business. He brought with him to Knole a Malay crease (or dagger) which Caraboo with great animation recognised as belonging to her country; and her desire to have it in her own possession was extreme, but from prudence it was denied her; this denial seemed only to increase her desire. She placed the dagger to her right side (where the Malays wear it) which confirmed this gentleman, that she perfectly understood the custom, though not the language of that country. In fencing she was particularly expert. Mr W. who esteemed himself a tolerable fencer when young, could seldom disarm her when using the long sword. At times she exercised herself with a sword in the right hand and a dagger in the left...

She, in truth, conducted herself so correctly, and her manners were so fascinating, that she soon became caressed and perfectly domesticated at Knole. She waited on Mrs W. at her toilette, and indeed had the whole range of the house; books of different descriptions, brought or procured for the purpose of ascertaining who she was, were constantly left in her way, and from these she read, and, no doubt, copied the characters which she wrote.

The grand lever, however, by which she performed all her deceptions, was, her own native English, which she could and did distinctly hear and profit by, tho' she never spoke it. Another singular key to deception was her astonishing command of countenance and self-possession. A jocose clerical gentleman of Bath tried to move her by flattery: he drew his chair close to her, looked steadily and smilingly in her face, and observed 'You are the most beautiful creature I ever beheld. You are an angel.' – Not a muscle of her face moved; no blush suffused her cheek; her countenance was motionless.

After three weeks residence at Knole, she was one morning missing. The *cacoethes errandi* [passion for roaming] had returned upon her, and she was panting for the shores of America. She had accordingly decamped; but returning again in the evening with a bundle of clothes, and her shoes and hands dirty, she gave Mrs W. and her servants to understand that she had dug them up from a place where she had buried them, to hide them from the Macratoos!

The truth was, that during her short absence she had hastened to Bristol; but fearing she might be pursued from Mrs W.'s, she cut across the country, by the Duchess of Beaufort's woods at Stoke, making her way through hedges, and over ditches, till she reached her old landlady's house in Lewins Mead, Bristol. From thence, packing up a trunk which she had left in her care, she ran to the Quay to look for a ship, the captain of which she had been in treaty with for her passage to America, before she set out on her vagrant expedition to Almondsbury; but the vessel had sailed! Returning to her lodgings, she paid her arrears of rent, had her trunk conveyed into Thomas Street, sent it to her father by one of the Exeter waggons, and returned with her bundle of clothes to Knole, with all possible expedition. Was it a wonder the girl should have been foot-sore and sick?

Having disposed of her heavy baggage she had nothing to look to but herself and bundle, and was thus ready for a march at a moment's notice, whenever circumstances occurred which were likely to lead to detection.

Soon after her return she was taken very ill, and the attendance of a respectable medical gentleman of Bristol was necessary. This gentleman had also been in the East, but during the painful hours of sickness, she contrived to elude even his scrutinizing endeavours to discover her country and language.

During her illness, in the presence of Mrs W. and two medical men who came to visit her, one suspicious circumstance certainly arose: it suddenly occurred to one of them to try the effect of alarming her, by stating to Mrs W. her extreme danger, and that it was probable she could not survive twenty-four hours longer; when in an instant her face became crimsoned. This circumstance, however, lost much of its weight from the maid who constantly attended her stating that such flushings had taken place five or six times every day during the continuance of her illness; an occurrence very common in typhus fever.

Disappointed in her intended escape to America, she appears to have reconciled herself to stay a little longer under Mrs W.'s protection. But whether she grew tired of the confinement at Knole, whether she dreaded discovery from the frequent visits she paid to Bristol in company with Mrs W. when she might chance to meet the eye of her old landlady, of Lewins Mead, or whether she heard under Mrs W.'s own roof of an intention of sending her to London, to be examined at the East India House; or under whatever apprehensions she may have laboured, she began to meditate another escape. And on Saturday the 6th of June, she again took her flight.

Mrs W. undoubtedly felt much uneasiness at her disappearance. She had as before taken with her not a pin or a ribbon which did not belong to her. Indeed her principles of honesty have been found unimpeachable, in whatever situation of life she has been discovered. It was towards Bath that she had now bent her way; and on the following Sunday Mrs W. received information of the place to which her protegée had flown. She again determined to reclaim her, and Mrs W. reached Bath on Sunday afternoon.

Here she found the Princess at the very pinnacle of her glory and ambition, in the drawing-room of a lady of *haut ton*. Cervantes himself could not have expected the realization of so fine a scene. What was the situation of Sancho Panza at the Palace of the Duchess, in comparison with the Princess of Javasu in the drawing-room of Mrs —— ? ... The girl afterwards declared, that this was the most trying scene she ever encountered, and that on this occasion she had more difficulty to refrain from laughing, and escape detection, than in all the singular occurrences of her life...

Dr Wilkinson of Bath, was another of the *cognoscenti* who was led likewise by the same love of the marvellous, which had duped so many other of the visitants at Knole, to try his skill at developing the character and nation of the unknown foreigner. And the publicity which the Doctor gave to his visit by detailing in the public prints [newspapers] a description of her person, manners, and situation was eventually the means of leading to a detection of the imposture...

The unexpected arrival of Mrs W. in the drawing room in Russell Street, Bath, was another occurrence which severely put to the test the girl's ingenuity and self-command. Mrs W. burst suddenly into the room, and in an instant Caraboo recognised her benefactress. She fell on her knees with that graceful prostration which she so well and so frequently practised, and embraced Mrs W. with an ardour of attachment and an appearance of joy and gratitude, which captivated every spectator.

She seemed to have forgotten the brilliancy of the scene around her, and as if overpowered by the ingratitude she had shown in leaving Mrs W.'s roof, she rushed through the company, and in an instant disappeared. She was followed down stairs by Mrs W. and when she found herself alone with her in the parlour below, she had the address again to reconcile Mrs W. to her escape, by making her believe, it was her anxiety alone to re-visit her parents at Javasu, which induced her to run away.

Mrs W. left Bath with Caraboo in her company the same night; and the relation to Mrs W. of the girl's exploits in the drawing-room, the commendations of such a host of spectators, aided by her apparently contrite expressions of sorrow, served to rivet stronger than ever the regard of Mrs W., and to convince her that her protegée was indeed an unfortunate Princess of Javasu.

Far different must have been the conflict of feelings passing at this time in the bosom of Caraboo herself. Proud of, and conscious, that on this occasion her powers of deception had surpassed all former exertions, she was at the same time equally conscious, that as her fame was extending, the hour could not be far off when the development [unfolding] of such a scene of duplicity must arrive. She had heard at Knole that the newspapers contained a description of her person and conduct, and an invitation to the public to interest themselves in her behalf; she felt that suspicion might be awakened as well as sympathy.

Her tears at Bath were the first symptoms of alarm and compunction which she betrayed; and on the Monday morning, after her return to Knole, Mrs W. observed her, not without some degree of surprise and apprehension, turn the lock of the chamber-door, after she entered Mrs W.'s dressing-room. Her heart misgave her at this moment; and Mrs W. has not now a doubt upon her mind, but that at this period the girl meditated an acknowledgment of the duplicity of her conduct. The occurrence nevertheless passed by, without any remark from Mrs W., and Caraboo resumed her usual cheerfulness throughout the day. The bubble, however, was on the eve of bursting.

The re-publication in the *Bristol Journal* of Dr Wilkinson's first letter led to the detection. Mrs Neale, with whom Caraboo had been lodging, read in that newspaper, with no little surprise and amusement, the freaks of Caraboo; and in an instant recognised the character of her *quondam* lodger. On Monday morning she called upon Mr Mortimer, and informed that gentleman of her suspicions, and produced such irrefragable proofs of her knowledge of Caraboo, that Mr M. the same evening thought it prudent to communicate the intelligence to Mrs W.; and singular to relate, before Mr M. left the parlour at Knole, a youth arrived from Westbury, the son of a wheelwright there, who had met with the girl on her first expedition to Knole, and who well remembered that, when in his company, spirits and water were not quite so repugnant to her taste as they had been at Knole.

This double disclosure flashed immediate conviction on Mrs.W.'s mind, and coupling these occurrences with the agitation of Caraboo in the morning, Mrs W. did not now hesitate to probe such suspicions to the bottom. She accordingly determined to wear the same appearance of friendship and kindness towards Caraboo during the evening, and in the morning to take her to Bristol and confront her with Mrs Neale.

Under the idea that she was going to Mr Bird's to finish the sitting for her portrait, which that gentleman was painting, she accompanied Mrs W. to that city, and they alighted at the appointed time at Mr Mortimer's, instead of Mr Bird's.

The discovery was speedy and decisive. Mrs W. having conversed with Mrs Neale and her daughters went alone into a room with Caraboo, told her of the damning proofs she had now obtained of her being an impostor, and after having tried once more in her gibberish to interest Mrs W. by saying 'Caraboo, Toddy, Moddy (father and mother) Irish,' she found she could not succeed; and Mrs W. being about to order Mrs Neale up stairs, she acknowledged the cheat; begging that Mrs W. would not cast her off, or suffer her father to be sent for. This Mrs W. promised upon certain conditions; one of which was, that she would instantly give a faithful detail of her former course of life, disclose her real name, her parentage and history.

'Caraboo' now told a long and pitiful story of the previous ten years. Her name was Mary Baker, born at Witheridge in 1791, but her parents' name was Wilcocks. (Her baptism was recorded at Witheridge on 23 November 1791, 'daughter of Thomas Wilcocks, shoemaker, almsperson [i.e. dependent on parish relief] by Mary his wife'.)

She had had a difficult relationship with her father, who had on a least one occasion flogged her. Then there were spells of service, sometimes paid just 10 pence a week, spells of begging or in hospital, service in London with a Mrs Matthews who had taught her to read, then a marriage, conducted by a Catholic priest, to a man who promptly deserted her. She had given birth to a child which was taken in at the Foundling Hospital, but died in its first year.

On the journey which first took her to Almondsbury, in her exotic but inexpensive dress, she was not seeking the attention of the gentry since they might well see through her disguise. Her initial reluctance to enter Knole was not feigned.

Since the book which tells us about her was published in 1817, immediately after her exposure, it includes nothing of her later life, but some things are known.

After her exposure, the kind Mrs Worrall paid for her to go to America, where she is thought to have acted 'Princess Caraboo' in freak shows, but never made much money. She returned to London around 1824, hiring a booth where people could view the Princess for a shilling a time, but neither there nor later in Bristol was her show a success.

On 28 September 1828 in Bedminster, which is part of Bristol south of the river, she married Richard Baker, ten years older than herself, but she did so using her mother's maiden name, as Mary Burgess. Why was it that she had called herself Mary Baker, or sometimes Mary Bakerstendht, in 1817? One can only speculate: perhaps her relationship with Richard Baker had begun much earlier, and he was married; perhaps the story of her Catholic marriage was an invention; or just possibly the whole thing was coincidence.

In the 1841 census Richard and Mary Baker and their 12 year old daughter Mary Anne were living in Hollybrook Place, Bedminster, where Richard is described as a 'leech dealer'. He supplied the local hospital. Leeches for blood-letting were considered vital as late as the 1930s, and indeed have become crucial once again as part of transplant surgery. Demand in Victorian times was so great that they had to be imported, and became an endangered species in Britain.

When Richard died in 1842 Mary took over his business. She too was a 'dealer in leeches', living in Princess Street, until her death aged 73 on Christmas Eve 1864, after which their daughter Mary Anne continued the family business. When the daughter died in 1900 she had saved enough to own four houses and had money in the bank.

In later life Mary had been ashamed of her Caraboo years, and did not wish to talk about it. A steady trade in blood-suckers was much more respectable. What a superb spy she would have made!

Or novelist?

Some other Bossiney books which might interest you

Druids in the South West?   Paul White

Between about 1740 and 1860 it was widely believed that 'the Druids' had built the stone circles of Dartmoor and Cornwall, and even what we now know are natural rock formations, such as the Cheesewring. How did the mistake occur? And who really *were* the Druids? A serious book which will make you laugh.

West Country Scandals   James Whinray

A bigamous duchess, an actress who ensnared a teenage Prince of Wales, three self-proclaimed Messiahs – these scandalous stories shocked (and entertained) previous generations but now throw light on the past.

How Devon changed the World – a bit   Paul White

From the first steam engine to the first commercial Christmas card, from central heating to the importation of tobacco, Devon ingenuity has produced some remarkable results – not all of them beneficial.

Weirdest Buildings of the West Country   Robert Hesketh

A chapel sprouting from the rocks, the last castle built in England (in the twentieth century), a pub built like a pack of cards, a lighthouse built on stilts – the West Country has more than its fair share of architectural oddities worth visiting.

Devon Smugglers   Robert Hesketh

Between 1700 and 1850, smuggling was a huge industry in Devon, actively supported by members of all social classes, but it was not romantic. This book gives a balanced view of 'free trade'.

Book Lover's Devon   Paul White

Features writers born in Devon as well as writers who settled in the county or took holidays which influenced their work – the famous (Jane Austen, Dickens, Agatha Christie) as well as some now largely forgotten. There are quite a few surprises, from Disraeli to Beatrix Potter.